First World War
and Army of Occupation
War Diary
France, Belgium and Germany

33 DIVISION
Divisional Troops
F Squadron North Irish Horse
16 November 1915 - 31 May 1916

WO95/2413/1

The Naval & Military Press Ltd
www.nmarchive.com
Published in association with The National Archives

Published by

The Naval & Military Press Ltd

Unit 10 Ridgewood Industrial Park,

Uckfield, East Sussex,

TN22 5QE England

Tel: +44 (0) 1825 749494

www.naval-military-press.com

www.nmarchive.com

This diary has been reprinted in facsimile from the original. Any imperfections are inevitably reproduced and the quality may fall short of modern type and cartographic standards.

© **Crown Copyright**
Images reproduced by permission of The National Archives, London, England, 2015.

Contents

Document type	Place/Title	Date From	Date To
Heading	WO95/2413/1		
Heading	33rd Division Divl Troops 'F' Sqdn Nth Irish Horse Nov 1915-May 1916 10 Corps		
Heading	33 "F" Sq N.I. Horse Vol 4		
Heading	33rd Division F Sq N.I. Horse Vol I Nov 15		
Heading	War Diary F. Squadron North Irish Horse D-M-T 33rd Div From 16 Nov. 1915 To 30th Nov. Volume I		
War Diary		16/11/1915	19/11/1915
War Diary	Morbecque	20/11/1915	30/11/1915
Heading	33rd Division F. Sq N. Irish Horse Vol 2		
Heading	War Diary. F. Squadron North Irish Horse 33rd Div		
War Diary	Le Cauroy	01/12/1915	31/12/1915
Heading	F Sq. N. Irish Horse Vol 3 Jan 10		
Heading	War Diary Of F Squadron North Irish Horse From 1st Jan 1916-31st Jan 1916		
War Diary		01/01/1916	31/01/1916
Heading	War Diary "F" Squadron North Irish Horse February 1916		
War Diary		01/02/1916	29/02/1916
Heading	War Diary "F" Squadron North Irish Horse 33rd Div March 1916 Vol 5		
War Diary		01/03/1916	31/03/1916
Heading	War Diary "F" Squadron North Irish Horse 33rd Division April 1916 Vol 6		
War Diary		01/04/1916	30/04/1916
Heading	War Diary "B" Squadron North Irish Horse 10th Corps May 1916		
War Diary		01/05/1916	31/05/1916

Disc 2/24/3 (1)
10:09am

Disc 2/21/3
9:50am

33RD DIVISION
DIVL TROOPS

'F' SQDN NTH IRISH HORSE
NOV 1915 – MAY 1916

10 CORPS

23

"F" Sq: N.I. Horse
Vol: 4

33rd Hussars

F.S: M.I. Horse
Vol. I

121/7634

Nov. 15.

Army Form C. 2118.

WAR DIARY
or
INTELLIGENCE SUMMARY.
(Erase heading not required.)

Instructions regarding War Diaries and Intelligence Summaries are contained in F. S. Regs., Part II. and the Staff Manual respectively. Title pages will be prepared in manuscript.

Hour, Date, Place / Summary of Events and Information	Remarks and references to Appendices
War Diary. ₹ Squadron North Irish Horse D-M-T 33rd Divⁿ From 16 Novʳ 1915 to 30ᵗʰ Novʳ Volume I	

WAR DIARY
or
INTELLIGENCE SUMMARY.
(Erase heading not required.)

Army Form C. 2118.

Hour, Date, Place	Summary of Events and Information	Remarks and references to Appendices
9.30 A.M. 16th Nov. 15	Left Netheravon & entrained at Amesbury. arrived Southampton 3-30 p.m. 4 horses cast of change. Embarked Western Miller sailed 5 p.m.	MK-W
6 A.M. 17th Nov. 15.	Arrived Havre. Disembarked. all well no casualties full complement men and horses. ordered to No 2. Camp. arrived 3 p.m. men in tents - very cold - received orders to entrain Nov 18th destination unknown.	
10 A.M. 18th Nov. 15.	Left No 2. Camp Havre. entrained 12 midday. Left HAVRE 3 p.m. Long slow journey 3 hours late - given no time to feed or water horses had to feed in the train.	
1 p.m. 19th Nov. 15.	Arrived Thiennes. detrained all well. arrived Morbecque 4 p.m. Billeted in 4	

WAR DIARY
or
INTELLIGENCE SUMMARY.
(Erase heading not required.)

Army Form C. 2118.

Instructions regarding War Diaries and Intelligence Summaries are contained in F.S. Regs., Part II. and the Staff Manual respectively. Title pages will be prepared in manuscript.

Hour, Date, Place	Summary of Events and Information	Remarks and references to Appendices
20th Nov Morbecque	Farms fairly comfortable.	
21st Nov. "	Visited HQrs 33rd Div. Sent groom to Gen. Landon's horse. Met major Gen. Gough at lunch an our hrs commander. Squadron inspected by Gen Gough, all well. Very cold. 2 hrs views orders to get ready to move.	MSS-IV
11 AM 22nd Nov. 9 AM 23rd Nov?	Proceeded by much road to near Bushes. arrived at 1.30 pm Had to leave 1 horse with fever on the way. march held up at Thiennes by Lahore Division.	

Army Form C. 2118.

WAR DIARY
or
INTELLIGENCE SUMMARY.
(Erase heading not required.)

Hour, Date, Place	Summary of Events and Information	Remarks and references to Appendices
24th	Two White near Busnes at le Cornet Bourdois. reported around to 33rd Division.	MS-N
25th	Nothing further	MS-N
26th	Nothing further Reconnoissance in direction of HAM.	MS-N MS-N

WAR DIARY
or
INTELLIGENCE SUMMARY.
(Erase heading not required.)

Army Form C. 2118.

Hour, Date, Place	Summary of Events and Information	Remarks and references to Appendices
27th Nov	Route March. Coming back died w/Pm march. no men fell out 10 miles.	MS-N
28th	Divine Service. Genl Lurgan was present	MS-N
29th	Road Reconnaissance. Report sent to G.S.O 33rd Div - Orders received to move to Le Cauroy.	MS-N
30th	Moved by march route to Le Cauroy. arrived 11pm. Billets fair.	MS-N

33 h/o Klwain

F.fr. N. 142 fever
vol: 2

124/791

Army Form C. 2118.

WAR DIARY
or
INTELLIGENCE SUMMARY.
(Erase heading not required.)

Hour, Date, Place	Summary of Events and Information	Remarks and references to Appendices
Dec. 1914	War. Diary. F. Squadron. North Irish Horse. 33rd Div? M Braunston Newman. Major F. Squadron N. I. H. 1st Jan? 1916.	

Instructions regarding War Diaries and Intelligence Summaries are contained in F. S. Regs., Part II. and the Staff Manual respectively. Title pages will be prepared in manuscript.

Army Form C. 2118.

WAR DIARY
or
INTELLIGENCE SUMMARY.
(Erase heading not required.)

Instructions regarding War Diaries and Intelligence Summaries are contained in F.S. Regs., Part II. and the Staff Manual respectively. Title pages will be prepared in manuscript.

Hour, Date, Place	Summary of Events and Information	Remarks and references to Appendices
1st Dec. CAVALRY	Routine duties	MAS-N
2nd Dec.	"	MAS-N
3rd Dec.	Huns dropped A.O.V.C.	MAS-N
4th Dec.	Road maintenance of all routes to concentration area at COMBE.	MAS-N
5th Dec.	Sundry duties. Divisions returned to billeting areas.	MAS-N
6th Dec.	Routine duties	MAS-N

Army Form C. 2118.

WAR DIARY
or
INTELLIGENCE SUMMARY.
(Erase heading not required.)

Instructions regarding War Diaries and Intelligence Summaries are contained in F. S. Regs., Part II. and the Staff Manual respectively. Title pages will be prepared in manuscript.

Hour, Date, Place	Summary of Events and Information	Remarks and references to Appendices
7th Dec.	Reconnaissance in environs of St Venant.	MSS-W
8th Dec.	Routine duties.	MSS-W
9th Dec.	Routine duties & lecture on Trench discipline.	MSS-W
10th Dec.	Orders received to move on 12th to CANTRAINE	MSS-W
11th Dec.	Routine duties	MSS-W
12th Dec.	Proceeded by march route to CANTRAINNE arrived about midday. Billets reasonable & most of the horses under cover. Came through big floods but all the transport was safely got in.	MSS-W

Army Form C. 2118.

WAR DIARY
or
INTELLIGENCE SUMMARY.
(Erase heading not required.)

Instructions regarding War Diaries and Intelligence Summaries are contained in F. S. Regs., Part II. and the Staff Manual respectively. Title pages will be prepared in manuscript.

Hour, Date, Place	Summary of Events and Information	Remarks and references to Appendices
13th Dec.	Three Officers & N.C.O.s proceeded to Lewis gun school at BUSNES.	MA-N
14th	Routine duties. Marked improvement of Horses	MA-N
15th } Dec?	9 Drawn's mine sunk to have standard B.	
16th		
17th		
18th		
19th "	Routine duties.	MS-N
20th "		MM-N
21st "	Marching out parade. Squadron went worth & kit & Transport at 11 am (Two hours).	
22nd "	Routine duties.	MS-N

(73989) W4141—463. 400,000. 9/14. H.&J.Ltd. Forms/C. 2118/10.

Army Form C. 2118.

WAR DIARY
or
INTELLIGENCE SUMMARY.
(Erase heading not required.)

Instructions regarding War Diaries and Intelligence Summaries are contained in F.S. Regs., Part II. and the Staff Manual respectively. Title pages will be prepared in manuscript.

Hour, Date, Place	Summary of Events and Information	Remarks and references to Appendices
23 Dec?	Combined scheme with Cyclists.	M6-N
24th "	Routine duties	M4-N
25th "	Church Parade.	M4-N
26th "	Routine duties	M4-N
	ditto.	
27th "	Troop schemes.	M4-N
28th "	Routine duties.	M4-N
29th "	Routine duties.	M5-N
30th "	Proceeded by march route to BEAUVRY at 10.30 A.M. arriving BEAUVRY 2.30 P.M. Transport came from SOUTH IRISH HORSE.	M4-N
31st "	Routine duties. Cleaning up camp &c.	M5-N

(7.3989) W4141—463. 400,000. 9/14. H.&J.Ltd. Forms/C. 2118/10.

Confidential

War Diary of F Squadron North Irish Horse
from 1st Jan 1916 — 31st Jan 1916.

[signature]
Major N.I. Horse
31st Jan 1916

Army Form C. 2118.

WAR DIARY
or
INTELLIGENCE SUMMARY.
(Erase heading not required.)

Instructions regarding War Diaries and Intelligence Summaries are contained in F. S. Regs., Part II and the Staff Manual respectively. Title pages will be prepared in manuscript.

Hour, Date, Place	Summary of Events and Information	Remarks and references to Appendices
Saturday 1st /Jan 1916	Routine duties	
2nd "	Church Parade.	
3rd "	Routine duties. musketry	
4th "	"	
5th "	"	
6th "	"	
7th "	"	
8th "	"	
11th "	Trenches. Section I.O.	
12th "	"	
13th "	"	
14th "	"	
15th "	no casualties.	
16th "		
17th "		

Army Form C. 2118.

WAR DIARY
or
INTELLIGENCE SUMMARY.
(Erase heading not required.)

Instructions regarding War Diaries and Intelligence Summaries are contained in F.S. Regs., Part II. and the Staff Manual respectively. Title pages will be prepared in manuscript.

Hour, Date, Place	Summary of Events and Information	Remarks and references to Appendices
18th Jan.	Routine duties	
19th	"	
20th	81 remounts arrived.	
21st	allotted remounts - routine duties.	
22nd	Routine duties	
23rd	Church Parade.	
24th	Routine duties	
25th	Routine duties	MS-W-
26th	"	
27th	" } Squadron usually now short ratio	
28th	Squadron drill.	
29th	Church Parade	
30th	Troop drill	
31st	Troop drill.	

WAR DIARY
"F" SQUADRON
NORTH IRISH HORSE
February 1916.

WAR DIARY
or
INTELLIGENCE SUMMARY.
(Erase heading not required.)

Army Form C. 2118.

Instructions regarding War Diaries and Intelligence Summaries are contained in F.S. Regs., Part II. and the Staff Manual respectively. Title pages will be prepared in manuscript.

Hour, Date, Place	Summary of Events and Information	Remarks and references to Appendices
1st Feb	Troop Drill	M{c}Lewman
2nd Feb	Routine duties	
3rd Feb	Squadron Field Day	
4th Feb	Routine duties	
5th Feb	1 Sergt 46 men Special Reconnaissance duty, 2.1 Trenches	
6th Feb	Routine duties	
7th "	Troop Reconnaissance	
8th "	Routine duties	
9th "	Lecture etc.	
10th "	Divisional Field Day	
11th "	Guides to trenches	
12th "	" " Fresh patrol of 1 Sergt 6 men	
13th "	" " Fresh patrol of 1 Sergt 6 men to 2.1. Sector	

Army Form C. 2118.

WAR DIARY
or
INTELLIGENCE SUMMARY.
(Erase heading not required.)

Instructions regarding War Diaries and Intelligence Summaries are contained in F. S. Regs., Part II. and the Staff Manual respectively. Title pages will be prepared in manuscript.

Hour, Date, Place	Summary of Events and Information	Remarks and references to Appendices
14th Feb.	Guides to Trenches by night. Church parade	} [illegible]
15th Feb.	Guides to Trenches individually	
16th Feb.	Routine in Mess. Lecture.	
17th Feb.	[illegible]	[illegible]
18th	[illegible]	
19th	[illegible]	
20th	[illegible]	
21st	[illegible]	
22nd	ditto	
23rd	ditto	
24th	ditto	
25th	Routine [illegible] Lecture	
26th	[illegible]	
27th	[illegible]	
28th	[illegible]	
29th	[illegible]	

(73989) W4141—463. 400,000. 9/14. H.&J.Ltd. Forms/C. 2118/10.

33

F' N I Horse
Vol 5

War Diary

'F' Squadron North Irish Horse. 33rd Div.

March 1916

M Kennth Newman.
Maj. & SC North Irish Horse

Army Form C. 2118.

WAR DIARY
or
INTELLIGENCE SUMMARY.
(Erase heading not required.)

Instructions regarding War Diaries and Intelligence Summaries are contained in F.S. Regs., Part II and the Staff Manual respectively. Title pages will be prepared in manuscript.

Hour, Date, Place	Summary of Events and Information	Remarks and references to Appendices
1st March	Trench fatigue. Inspection 7 who helmets.	
2nd "	Trench fatigue	
3rd "	Training horsh riders	
4th "	Trench fatigue	
5th "	Routine duties	
6th "	"	
7th "	"	Mrs-N
8th "	fire inspection.	
9th "	field day. G.S. staff.	
10th "	Routine duties	
11th "	"	
12th "	Kit inspection - 55 remounts arrived	

Army Form C. 2118.

WAR DIARY
or
INTELLIGENCE SUMMARY.
(Erase heading not required.)

Instructions regarding War Diaries and Intelligence Summaries are contained in F.S. Regs., Part II and the Staff Manual respectively. Title pages will be prepared in manuscript.

Hour, Date, Place	Summary of Events and Information	Remarks and references to Appendices
13. March	Tuesday.	
14" "	Bathing parade	
15" "	Routine duties. No return snow kilmets.	
16" "	Tues day.	
17" "	Routine duties	
18th "	Tues Day "	
19th "	Church Parade.	NKS-N
20th "	Routine duties	
21st "	" "	
22nd "	" " no return snow kilmets.	
23rd "	" "	
24th "	Field Day	
25th "	Routine duties	
26th "	"	
27th "	Battn's Parade	

Army Form C. 2118.

WAR DIARY
or
INTELLIGENCE SUMMARY.
(Erase heading not required.)

Instructions regarding War Diaries and Intelligence Summaries are contained in F.S. Regs., Part II and the Staff Manual respectively. Title pages will be prepared in manuscript.

Hour, Date, Place	Summary of Events and Information	Remarks and references to Appendices
28th March	Full day	} Mks-N
29th "	Routine duties	
30th "	Full day	
31st "	Routine duties.	

Vol 6

War Diary.
"F" Squadron. North Irish Horse
33rd Division
April 1916.

Army Form C. 2118.

WAR DIARY
or
INTELLIGENCE SUMMARY.
(Erase heading not required.)

Instructions regarding War Diaries and Intelligence Summaries are contained in F.S. Regs., Part II and the Staff Manual respectively. Title pages will be prepared in manuscript.

Hour, Date, Place	Summary of Events and Information	Remarks and references to Appendices
1. April.	Exercise & Riding School. Sand Drill	
2. "	Church Parade	
3. "	Squadron Drill	
4. "	Inspection by A.O.v.S.	
5. "	Routine duties	
6. "	Reconnaissance in vicinity of ARRAS.	
7. "	Routine duties.	
8. "	Squadron drill. Kit inspection.	
9. "	Church Parade.	
10. "	Squadron Drill	
11. "	Routine duties	
12. "	Riding School Battery & horses	

WAR DIARY
or
INTELLIGENCE SUMMARY.
(Erase heading not required.)

Army Form C. 2118.

Hour, Date, Place	Summary of Events and Information	Remarks and references to Appendices
13 April.	Practise Ceremonial Parade.	
14 "	Ceremonial Parade BETHUNE	
15 "	Routine duties.	
16 "	Digging party to trenches.	
17 "	"	
18 "	Routine duties.	
19 "	Squadron probably march out to Coyecque. Issues.	
20 "		
21 "	Routine duties.	
22 "	Squadron drill & lecture.	
23 "	Routine duties.	
24 "	Field day. Lecture.	

Army Form C. 2118.

WAR DIARY
or
INTELLIGENCE SUMMARY.
(Erase heading not required.)

Instructions regarding War Diaries and Intelligence Summaries are contained in F. S. Regs., Part II. and the Staff Manual respectively. Title pages will be prepared in manuscript.

Hour, Date, Place	Summary of Events and Information	Remarks and references to Appendices
25 April.	Drill & lecture.	
26th "	Advance guard Scheme.	MK-W
27th "	" "	
28th "	Seizing of positions	
29th "	Publican hat at rest	
30th "	Church parade.	

Mulholland Newman
Major North Irish Horse

B.N.I.Hoze 33
Vol 5

War Diary
North Irish Horse
1st Corps.
10 May 1916.

[signature] Major.
O.C. 'B' Squadron North Irish Horse

'B' Squadron

Army Form C. 2118.

WAR DIARY
or
INTELLIGENCE SUMMARY.
(Erase heading not required.)

Instructions regarding War Diaries and Intelligence Summaries are contained in F. S. Regs., Part II. and the Staff Manual respectively. Title pages will be prepared in manuscript.

Hour, Date, Place	Summary of Events and Information	Remarks and references to Appendices
1st May 1916	Squadron at ISQUES near BOULOGNE attached 1st Cav'y Div'n for training. Advanced 9 Reinforcements Posted to 3 Div'ns	
2nd "	Routine duties. Lecture Pioneering	
3rd "	Night Concentration march. Lecture from C.R.A.	
4th "	Paraded drill HARDELOT. Construction Patrolling	
5th "	Scheme against Cavalry Brigade. Lecture.	MAY IV
6th "	Scheme against 2 Squadrons.	
7th "	Routine duties. Church Parade	
8th "		
9th "	Inspection Drill.	
10th "	Scheme	
11th "	Captains duties lectures	

WAR DIARY
or
INTELLIGENCE SUMMARY.

(Erase heading not required.)

Army Form C. 2118.

Hour, Date, Place	Summary of Events and Information	Remarks and references to Appendices
May 12th	Proceeded by march route to MARESQUEL.	
" 13th	" " " MONT CHEL.	
" 14th	" " " LAVIGOGNE hills	
" 15th	Horse markings Mounting duties	MMN
" 16th	Changed billets to VERT GALAND	
" 17th	Saddle inspection.	
" 18th	Troop drill.	
" 19th	Horseshow 49th Div?	
" 20th	Squadron proceeded by march route to SENLIS to join 32nd Div?	
" 21st	Mounted duties	
" 22nd	Diggins party to Corps cables 5.0 mis to trenches	

WAR DIARY or INTELLIGENCE SUMMARY.

(Erase heading not required.)

Army Form C. 2118.

Instructions regarding War Diaries and Intelligence Summaries are contained in F.S. Regs., Part II. and the Staff Manual respectively. Title pages will be prepared in manuscript.

Hour, Date, Place	Summary of Events and Information	Remarks and references to Appendices
23rd May.	Digging in trenches	
24th "	"	
25th "	4th Army relieved 3rd Army	
26th "	6th known as "B" Sqd instead of "F" Squadron	MMN
27th "	Established an O.P in trenches under Lieut Lowe + Sergt Brumsby.	
28th "	"	
29th "	"	
30th "	Relieved 2 Hotchkiss Guns Crew	
31st "	From under Lieut Lowe.	

www.ingramcontent.com/pod-product-compliance
Lightning Source LLC
Chambersburg PA
CBHW081500160426
43193CB00013B/2551